The Birth of Snow

Also by the Author

Remembering Rew (a chapbook)

Some Holy Weight in the Village Air (poems)

Songs from an Earlier Century (poems)

The Creek at the End of the Lawns (poems)

Wide and Wavy Out of Salamanca (essays)

The Birth of Snow

Poems

Ira Joe Fisher

Athanata Arts, Ltd.
New York

Published by Athanata Arts, Ltd.
152 Roxbury Road
Garden City, New York 11530

www.athanata.com

Published and printed in the United States of America

ISBN 979-8-9919585-0-9 (hardcover)
ISBN 979-8-9919585-1-6 (paperback)

First edition

Library of Congress Catalog Control Number: 2024949991

Interior and cover design: Kenji Liu

Cover art: Ira Joe Fisher

...for Nick Clooney: most intelligent, kindest, guiding newsman and anchor; gifted singer and raconteur, actor and emcee; devoted husband to Nina and father to Ada and George; and friend to us whose paths were blessed to follow for a time in your path. ...for all you have given to the world, to us, and ...to me, I dedicate this book.

You are a smiling treasure of a friend, Nicholas. You are in my heart.

Table of Contents

Snow,

if you fall in the dark,
wake me.
Needle the window.
Judder the streetlamp.
Beg the wind to wail
through boughs de-leafed
or swishing pines
forever green.
You're a tale
I can't bear missing.
So, snow,
if you fall in the dark,
wake me.

Apostrophe

Greetings, sheet of paper.
Empty, white, waiting, flat.
Like Manhattan,
you can do very well
without me.
Like a meadow pond,
I want to dip
into your untouched stillness
and ink wrinkles
across your field,
your road, your glow.
O, sheet of paper,
Like a mine,
you keep your prospects
hidden dark beneath
a door-like light.
The bus, the boat, the key
to your rippling wisdom
is a pen hugged hoping
between my finger and my thumb.

Within the Pages of An Old Book

A lost marker burned a place
for God and the old poems
only know how many years.
The pages are creased beneath
the withered, bending cover,
its seeping stain dried, jaggéd;
thread frays from the blunt corner.

Who bought this book sixty years
ago? Someone to raise it,
praise it, graze it, exalt it
with her devouring eyes.
How many since have cracked it
And sung its singed silent songs?
One reader marked the pages
where she last left off and hoped,
I hope, to return.

That found bookmark burned into
the pages. And opening
this dusty, aged and wordy
weight settles light on verses
that long languished in a tight,
waiting, airless dark for God
and the poems only know
how many years.

Question

If I were to sleep upon a poem,
Would its song seep into me?

Book Learning

Summer bakes the printer's shop
in the dark morning
with the smell of kerosene and ink.

Two presses hum and tap time away.
Silver lead letters cool to words
and shape all we'll ever know

of Annville, of the world.
A book builds with a slugged, galley heft.
Proof the type and the inky slivers
and measured folds and licorice ink and gray men

wearing aprons. They swear and laugh
as ditch-diggers do. They swear, they laugh
but they weigh words and wisdom
And that wisdom rises
out of the shop, into the world.

Poem on the Wall

Every night ahead of slumber
As I feel conscious unencumber
Me in day that now is night
I look upon a poem
That hangs upon my wall.
In the dark its paper dims
The words to a ghostly sight.
And through the pass where
The shade can't get together with the sill
A blade of light falls upon the words.
It's from a lamp in the yard
To keep the thieves away,
Yet this very guardian ray
Sneaks uninvited into my room
As dust or a moth might.
This light is on the poem
That hangs upon the wall
And makes the poster poem
Seem misty and quite small.
Its words spill over
And make of love a river
That flows where it must,
Leaving some in every day
And place along its way,
Attracting more, drawing more
Streaming in a moving pace.

If a lamp cannot illuminate
A love poem's every trait
Its mission is a mission lost
And what is spent is just its cost.

Unforgiving

Time grinds with a grasping friction
Like the carve of a creek in rocks.

Time a-crueling and time aging.
Time scars rocks with igneous pocks

As it flows and froths from the deep.
Roiling sepia can't-be-seen

On its way to a deeper seep,
Spoil'd, raking, bent on being mean.

Free

The snowflakes aren't falling,
they're floating,
rolling,
playing
in the pine-shadowed day.
Snowflakes reluctant
to end their frost-kissed
tumbling
through the biting air,
reluctant
to lock
their pieces of heaven
upon earth,
to end their giddy descent
as shackled gems
with nothing to do
but sparkle.

Propinquity

The mountains around Annville
are never blue.
Even when it rains.
Winter scars them gray
against the white snow.
But, they're not mountains;
they're hills.
And the Annville hills
are never far enough away
to be blue.

A Smudge of Clouds

A smudge of clouds,
A stain...
...of rain.

Betrayal

The rain drips sad upon the snow.
The night-married gray cruelly dims
December's diamonds.
And dims the songs, the Christmas hymns.

The bare, veiny trees reach higher
To invite thawing by clawing
At the cloud-hefted sky,
At wintering air see-sawing

From chill to mild, from melt to freeze
More like a budding, marching air
That speaks of burst and bird,
Not a boned-cold breathe-if-you-dare.

Storm Overture

The rumble of the mower fogs
Along the lawn. A dump truck clanks

Along Governor Street, scraping
From gear to gear. It wrests me

From the leaves applauding the wind,
Wrests me from bluebird and finch.

I only need a drowsy day,
A waving pine, a small death breath

of lilacs beside a peeling
wall to ride upon sunny dust

to the top of the round maple.
I only need a slope 'bove town.

I only need the blue rag puffs
of a climbing cumulous cloud

like shadows on snow. Thunder from
the fading side of the hilly

trees comes spying. Cicadas spin
their rattling sputter-song.

The little dog sleeps. A child sits
in the clover lawn and he knows,

wisely knows, that the storm will storm.
And he'll think of this forever.

Low Clouds of Late Winter

Low clouds of late winter
draw light from the city,
smooth it, diffuse it
and color it orange.

In the deep night with no moon
each tree stands distinct.
Each rock bulges brown
out of the hill.

The road, in a glowing rain,
curves and climbs and falls
in lines of rutted slush.
Rain slants in the street lamp light,

and crackles on the roof.
Snow – white Gypsy curtain beads –
is gone from the air.
It steams on the ground,

pounded by the rain,
and in the refracted city light,
it's faintly the color of blood.

Poor Man's Music

"...and the old church tower,
Whose bells, the poor man's only music, rang
From morn to evening, all the hot Fair-day..."
FROM "FROST AT MIDNIGHT" BY SAMUEL TAYLOR COLERIDGE

What is it about a village
where noon sounds a siren
that drowns the church bell?
Fear of fire?
Fear of faith?
What is it about a village
whose ghosts rise wrinkled
in dust, in dusk after begging
of the dark some rest?
What is it about a village
With a belfry sitting higher
than the horns
on the fire house roof.
Higher, brighter
and begging day
to notice,
to change,
to cup
the worker's ear
at the tavern door,
and turn, instead,
to the willows bowing
by the creek and shuddering

sun on cobbles,
begging like bells
with the wobbling water.
Begging the village
to slow,
to stretch the moment,
to hear the tired ghosts
trying to rise
through a siren
drowning a church bell.
What is it about a village
and its stones
beside the road
running away like deep river?
Stones sitting,
splintering light;
stones working up
through earth
or down, down

in a fallen star.
Stones in the freeze
and heave of winter;
in disked and drilled spring
and stones
that rode a boat
from the harrowed field.
What is it about the village bells

and the creek joining
the sparrow and the finch
and the barn-swallow
to dip their liquid song
from water
and sky to pour down
on the sunburned worker,
pour down on the girl beside the cow
clomping back
to the barn,
pour down on the hill
above the village
in the misty valley.
And the song, the song
can never settle
in the air.

Chiaroscuro

How magic that a beam of light
Pools on the leaf,
Softens the veins and green
And falls as shade to the grass below.
How magic.

Out of Sound

In my room where poems rag
and rake the air for notice;

where photos of Lincoln and Frost
look sternly out on things,

where tree-slim Saint Francis rises
beside a mug stained with drizzle.

In the room where torn, shiny books
clutter floor to ceiling,

there is no nearby window for listening
to the rain. I have a radio

and downstairs the playing
of my children. But I wish the rain

could reach me with its dropped,
broken notes rilling down the shingles.

I want the rain to give some wet heaven
to an earth-dirtied day.

The Children's Game

A sparrow stops in a hop
 on the fence around a park;
the challenge of children's bingo
plays out in the dimming day.

Like bubbles just before they pop
the children play ahead of dark.
Does the bird wish to mingle?
She twitches with something to say.

But the children's game doesn't stop,
they're absorbed in their own lark.
(Neither spoke the other's lingo).
And the sparrow flies away.

My Youth

Wait, wait, wait …I wasn't through with it yet.
I put it down to buy a house and turned to pick it up
And it was gone. Stolen. Spirited over the hill.
There were still things I wanted to see
And girls I wanted to kiss.

Cycling

Dust puffs from the wheel of my brother's
bike over the dirt road, the back way

into Salamanca. I peddle hard. Hanging oak
leaves carve a tunnel over stones popping

August beneath our tires. My brother
waits at the top of each hill; I wobble

and sweat in the now-and-then sun shuddering
through the trees. He waits and frowns or he waits

and stares; but he waits; pale threads at the ends
of his sleeves wiggle with the wind. I ask

how many miles. He says the back way is ten.
My sock shows through the toe of one sneaker.

I wonder about rabbits in the tall grass
beside us. Do we scare them or just prove

we're fools? I've heard our father talk of cougars
and bears in the woods. My brother squints

and tells me he's seen them. Then he spits
in the dirt and climbs back on his bike.

I spit and climb back on mine. We coast downhill
past carrots and corn in poor-people gardens.

We coast by high weeds choking wrecked autos;
and roofs the color of rust. When we rest

on the hilltops we talk about baseball
and my brother's paper route and girls

I know he has kissed. I wonder
if he wonders if anyone noticed

we're gone. I don't ask. And my brother
doesn't say. This day this road hears only

the bicycles of two boys peddling
the back way into Salamanca.

Missed Moonlight

There is Brem who will explore love;
And Lottie who looks down to smile.
They'll give and they'll grasp the red hour
And meet deep, dreamless, all the while.

He of the bottle and hunger
And veiny, wide, powder-plowed eyes.
She teared from wadded, wrinkled notes;
Inky moons, inky sheets, good buys.

Each, the other will never know;
Yet, they'll scuff the same grounded dust.
Two grow into some sort of love
And two part into mere lone lust.

Fog Like an Old Man

The fog would not leave.
Like an old man at the diner
who scuffs in for coffee
and a cup of bean soup
and sits in the heat in courderoy and plaid,
the fog would not leave.
It had grayed two days
and dripped a rude intrusion
from street lamps. Trees split
the late light into spider webs
like the lines on the old man's face
as he rattles, un-read, the morning paper
hoping someone will speak
or ask his mind
on those bastards in Washington.

Now Known

Under heavy shoes the stairs creak.
Thin legs press each step with great care.
A parchment hand grips tight the rail.
The furrowed lips quiver and frown.
Edith passes through the sunlight
Tinted in stained-glass encounter.
She shuffles on the thread carpet
And – dwarfed by her old chair – she sits.
The outside pines invite blackbirds
And the wind to sing and to fly.
She, not hearing, can only sigh.
Age forbids the sounds to her ear.
Clouds converge and Edith's view dims.
Beyond, the birds calm; the wind grows.
The smalling old woman's eyes close.
Three days later another lid
will close. And what is seen ...or heard?

One December Day

Up back of the cinder-block house, a spring
Crazes the pines with ice. The snow-cold air
Hints at hoary magic. A creek, between
The pine spring and Eldon, judders so cold
And sparkling; afraid of stopping, afraid
Of freezing. A rusted old barbed wire dives
And rises from post to post in piled snow
Like an aged, unfeared serpent. Eldon's down
In the house blowing steam on the window
With his breathing. He's thinking he'll clump up
And lie by the spring in the pines. His hand
Wound 'round a shotgun, he recalls from when
He was a boy where to step in the snow,
On a path uphill to the soft, shushing,
Summoning pines where, with just one good squall,
He'll not be found until April.

The Call

It is all about woods.
Greened and gray and gold.

It is all about woods –
rising, spiky pine, bubbling

globes of leaves on hills
soaring round and making a valley.

And wind, always wind –
soft or roaring in the trees.

It is about hearing the call,
hearing the call and responding.

The trunks of the trees are lined,
grooved, etched with age.

Arm-like branches,
twigs like fingers.

And a boy in sun says
I am going up into the woods.

For berries and to lie upon the moss,
to hear jays and swallows and wrens.

A boy is all about woods
whited and cracked and dark

to slide his sled upon the snow.
Snow blue-shadowed and deep.

The woods call in dark or day
and wait for the few, for the one

who will hear and answer
the call to the woods.

The Map of Winter

The creek behind the house is becoming
a creek again, water is swelling it.
Lazy water that is yet more mirror
Than burble beneath the still leafless trees.
The map of winter is being effaced.

Three robins find a feast in the browned ground.
The wind is lifted away from the earth
And plays its mischief high in the cirrus
Serious clouds o'er the low overcast.
The map of winter is being effaced.

Soon a latent green will sneak up and grow
And that green will weave with gold and the new
Air dusted and warm, laughing at jackets.
A forgetting will come to all the cold
And the map of winter will be effaced.

Tilted Mourning

Why, flag, do you droop?
Over the huge fireplace
Above a small flame
What is it, flag, you can't face?

Are you grieved at what you gloried?
Does the poet's rage
(Before our still, calm sitting)
At war you lead, at war you wage

Weigh you down, the weight of shame?
Or are you now two centuries tired
Of hate, of hurt, of killing,
Of crusades in which you're mired?

1-A

In third grade
I wanted
to carve a tomahawk
out of a piece of tagboard.

I flashed my mother's
paring knife.
It slipped

and sliced my finger.
The cut healed to a scar
noted on my draft card.

Perhaps

They don't speak.
She in white earrings
and he in a blue plaid shirt.
She bites her powdery roll.
He spears wet lettuce.
They don't speak.
They sip their beer
from delicate glasses, but
they don't speak.
Beneath blued hair
she picks with her fork
at the lumped special
on a blue plate,
raising her brows
like a surgeon.
And he – behind lenses
that shrink day to a square –
hunches over the meal
they've split
and chews as if that's all
he means to do,
as if he has no choice.
Perhaps the daughter won't listen.
Perhaps the son still drinks.
Because they don't speak.

Eighth of September

Stopped, my auto tings
as it settles in the train-station lot.
September keeps up a green-tree front;
but, autumn sends word
in the gray paper clouds
that it'll be pleased to have summer
leave. And soon. Look up
at the trees, through the leaves
at the pied-sky.
And in some old, sensed time,
this brief remembering
is more waving threads than woven cloth;
more blink than painted scene
or dream. And then, it all ends;
all ends as it began.
In a corner of the train-station lot.

A Case

The books on my bookshelf lean;
diff'rent lengths and thick or thin.

Off left the novel of drunks
in Spain stands straight, but three books

in (a tale of Northwest snow
and the death of a sailor)

the tipping begins; and hits
a sagged angle at mid-shelf,

beside that volume confused
with a truth and miracles

(its blue jacket nearly ripped
away). If the shelf were stuffed

and the air between as dead
as dust, how could I enter

the watery smoke and ghosts?
There'd be no air for haunting.

It's good for our books to sag,
to wobble and end up bent,

from a night-light and thumbing;
borrowing and being lent.

The books on my bookshelf lean;
and in their riffled, weary,

world-wrinkled spending, it's why
they're inked to do what they do.

The Birth of Snow

A Spark. Small as the point of a pin
Shines soft in a white cloud high above
Building, village, and farm. Then a water drop
Wraps the shining spark in cold and ice.
The arctic wind weaves that spark with more sparks
In the growing cloud – dark and descending
With winter's weight. Other winds flee the pole
(Where shadows are blue and sun's a stranger).
The whistling squalls brush the sea-big lakes
And draft empires of drops to freeze infinite
Sparks to chills, to glints and those sparks small
As points of pins grow in night-moans to icy
White and begin their tumble as snow.

December, Upstate

We see the black, the window mirrored, sucking up our talking.
It cools, it falls, it carries down the scuffs from all our walking.
The night can come, the air can freeze the moment winter-filling
with something begging to be seen and felt and killing.
There is no warming hand, no heating up or leaving
this pulling down, this shivered frown, this frosted thread,
this weaving.

Snow and a Leaf

Two graves. Among a thousand, under trees,
under leaves, under the early snow.
Two men: the blacksmith and the schoolmaster.
With the feathered snow, a here and there leaf
on the graves in the village, in the valley
between soft hills all the seasons visit.

The blacksmith's sons walked to his mounded grave.
They pushed their hands into their pockets;
Their shoulders squeezed up to warm their ears.
They look down at the snow their shoes disturb.
At the grave one wishes there were more trees.
Another hopes the stone is big enough
to be loving. They look at the blacksmith's name
and his birth-to-death years chiseled beneath.
The snow sucks the cold up into their shoes.
One son thinks about the blacksmith's arms
with tattoos blued and blurry. Another
thinks about his sunburned head where the gift
to fix anything lived. They're at the grave
that mounds beside the other mounding graves
in the village in the valley. Winter
was so eager it came in November.

A wooden house two leafy streets away
had an upstairs and a porch where seven
children played before it was surrendered
to jobs and blowing leaves. There was a kitchen

window, small, just above the sink, and it
wasn't until the kind schoolmaster died
and was given to the grave that his wife
discovered she could see his stone two streets
away. So now she could even count
on washing dishes to make her cry.

A Good Enough Heaven

The crippled branches sketch an old man's face.
He frowns off to the right. Twigs sketch a nose,
Broken in a gin mill and oil-field hockey.
A bumpy branch curves his forehead.
He peers out of a knot.

The wind wisps a squirrel's nest
Into an eyebrow, arching high in the tree
As it arched in life, in anger. This would be
A good enough heaven, a beech by
A creek, in the bud-lusty breeze, a good

Enough heaven for a man who worshipped the woods,
The billowing breath of an eight-point buck,
A pheasant spinning the earth; a hunt, a beer,
A snooze on the creek-side moss. Just a
Wind, warming rain, and an old man's

Face penciled in the trees. A good enough
Heaven for a fellow whose hope hovered just
Beyond the window, over the rippling pond,
Fog in the cowslip air. In drooping spring leaves
I see the old man's face.

Deceptive Winter

A thaw that came
and gave
the snow a melt
befell a similar fate:
it came,
was cooled
and lost the day
defeated
from its weight.

By Rights

This cold March day flaunts fog and rain
Causing complainiers to complain.

But, winter's still upon the date;
Spring isn't early, winter's late.

So, such grumbling dirties the air
When some snow, by rights, could be there.

Snow Knowledge

What can the snow know?
Does it dip and dart smart?
Will it choose to cover or hover
    seeking the coldest bed?

Could snow make the wind rescind
What its falling first thought sought
In crystal-washed tumbling and fumbling
    That grayed the sky to dread?

December Will Not Be Ignored

December will not be ignored
With its falling, squalling snow
Washing white on the twiggy trees
Closing the creek's troubled flow.

This twelfth of months rips at clouds,
With wind and shaking and spilling,
Iron cold and minor chord song
Sing of their sunshine killing.

Squinting its eye clouding with age,
Wrinkled winter cackles, teasing.
December, not to be ignored, holds
The air on the frozen side of freezing.

Look Out

You, first flakes of the blizzard, dance
In blithe ignoring of drifts to follow.
Wind whirls in the bluing air
While eyes in the houses and the woods
Look out and look out for the warring heft
That'll rage and rattle all the night.
Tomorrow the trees will fold snow
In their bark; snow swirling and needling
Twigs and foolish leaves and grayed windows.

Christmas Music

The holidays begin in wind.
Mysterious wind
with scents of cinnamon
and fir.
And night.
Old mystery night
ghosting clouds
across the moon.
These winter holidays,
these holy days all begin in wind
and night and snow.
Snow in the trees.
Snow in the heart.
Sparkled air ...cold.
Cold
And hope.
And bells and voices and music.
Christmas Music.
Affecting in a wintry way
and not mere longing.
Longing, yes; but, reaching further.
Further into time;
deeper *than* time.
More than just young days.
Christmas music reaches back
before you, before us.
It reaches deeper
than the day

the song was born and sung.
It ushers us to a dark enchantment:
old velvet cold,
wolves in the woods
and whispering snow,
whispering snow,
whooing wind,
and tumbling bells
beneath the sentient stars.
Christmas music stirs the smell of hay
and pines and feast.
We ride the music
on a moaning whipstick wind
through leaf-lost trees.
On that music we swirl
slow and warm.
And – for a green-wreathed moment –
the song hides us
from an angry world.
We leave the angry world
– for a few year-aging moments –
to touch, again, a place,
a force,
a scene,
a sky,
a flame,
a glow,
a gift,

a sigh,
a star,
a leaving and returning
to that with no higher name
…than peace.
We wish that, with no higher wish
…than peace.

Beg Pardon...

Sun, a word?
You're at work and melt on late winter.
Bless you.
The snow must go from flake to ice
to rivulet.
and you're about all that just now.

But, Sun,
could you radiate our sullen souls
Losing, lost?
Might you aim your beam and whaps
on evil
for a season, for a life, for ever?

I ask, old Sun,
I ask for the despair alive and licking
the dark
heart in me, in them, in all
who slog
in weary fear of the next bad, sad minute.

Your light,
Sun, your light might breathe and brighten
and bubble hope,
and wisp to cooling dust, to windy dust
a hate,
all hate and haughty hands on hips.

The kings
and killers whose blood is red, not blue;
whose hearts
cannot beat through the smoke and battle rattle
of dawn and dark
and the ears of trembling youth.

Terra Firma

I keep inland, away from the sea.
Waves sicken, the depth horrifies me.

Woods on all sides I sighingly seek;
Meadowsweet goldenrod by a creek.

I shy from the ocean and foamy brine
Dreading to venture past the tree line.

Escape

It seems I – who am afraid of flying – floated
Up and above your old, squat homes,
Over your treed hills and hilly trees,
Beyond the mossy banks of wiggling creeks.
I – afraid of flying – floated
Over the rising, waving sidewalks
Crumbling beside your heaving, winding streets;
Fluttering the grass in your yards
Behind those peeling-paint houses.
O, Annville, all this – you – I left:
Street lamps, kissing, and leaves,
Ball fields, folk songs, and barns.
Like a flitting swallow, I flew off
With the morning-gloried robins
Who gave their bird-beauty
To morning and farm,
Where barbed-wire fences countied
Cows, mapped their mooing
Out of the wakes of bicycle boys
Noticing the ignoring bicycle girls.
I floated high and away
Into the humid, curious air
Lusted by summer
Baking hay and lawns and hopes
For the flesh, for the heart
Forsaking holding, heating hands.

Dim Walk

I wonder how such white can be so bleak.
To think the sun yet lives is beyond me.
It may know of a place where sights are bright,
As there and elsewhere it is day or night.
The blued snow is stopped in its tidal plunge,
the arriving breeze urges it to lunge.
Snowdrifts have say over the air-chilled rush
to be cold and toss my cap into slush.
I'd rather call it winter's play, at that,
and dry the drops as I retrieve my hat.

The Day Before a Storm

A winter sun burns upon the window,
Upon my flannel back, upon my neck.
Sky cloudless and blue and icy high calm.

Coming evening is graced with breathy air
The color of empty, unused moments
In which I cannot gain a firm purchase.

The last storm lies wounded and pushed aside.
Jaggéd pieces of luminous defeat
Languish white and out of the sidewalk way.

Tomorrow's storm eyes east and arms with snow
Its unwearying wind already in
The woods, trembling and troubling gray trees.

The Four A.M. Snow

The light on the porch tumbles the storm,
Little white islands from continent clouds
Sheared in the dizzied dark from sky to ground.
The edge of the roof and the window corner
Draw winter in a black triangle
Against which the antic squall pokes the night.
I dream of learning fir-scented secrets.

To Some Older Folks

To some older folks
their youth is revealed
and back to days
the years have concealed
an observer is spirited
to images peeled
bare of the dim mist,
bare of time's shield.
Returning, the observer ponders
the weapon time wields,
inflicting its damage,
'til the funeral bell's pealed.

The Hill Behind

There's a spring bubbling up in the woods,
the air blue and hung with perfect round drops
cooling and breaking and ghosting away.

The pines are wet on the hill in the woods
and wet are the willows over the creek
behind the house Asa lived in to leave.

Winter muffled sound beneath the pines
and Asa broke the soft snow every day
at the out-of-breath end of his running.

The spring bubbled and sputtered all winter;
a straight slender vapor like cabin smoke
rose from a hole in the soot-spotted snow.

He kneeled and asked of the minstrel wind
to lift and carry him even deeper
into the thick woods, away and hidden.

Asa prayed in that place for a leafy space
under the trees, under the ferns; a place
too soft, too lost, too tucked for finding.

That trembling prayer lifted in a breath-fog
for the same bramble-hidden comfort
found by fox and rabbit and scared sparrow.

The wind could bow the strings of the pines
and hide the winter world that was lost, lost,
lost even in the snow-muffled spring.

The Quiet Rage of a Winter Storm

The quiet rage of a winter storm –
All swirls and curtained white –
Holds hands with the hands of the wind
And rides the snow from day into night.

A night of no stars and lumping heights
as the snow piles and sculpts.
Birds and squirrels tremble in leaf-nest fright.
Deer curve and hide from the white terror.

Dawn's limbs are lined a spidery white
As dawn clears to calm day
And look at the soft, sunny morning:
All the shadows are blue.

A Woman on the Train

The brakes scream as the New Haven train
bites the track at the station. I watch

a getting-off woman stagger in the aisle.
She grips a seatback and teeters

in the car wobbling into a stop.
Her wrinkle-waved hair frames

grey eyes and she glances about,
embarrassed. Is her name, I wonder,

Mary? Or Tasha? Or Missus Straight?
The flowered dress reaches to her ankles;

stockings and shoes are black. Her breathing
heaves her blue sweater and the gripping hand

looks no whiter than her hand hanging limp.
The train tips, slows, lurches, halts.

The woman – Helen? Prudence? Eve? –
strides out to the platform. If she needed to recover,

she has. And the train's fumey
breeze fingers her hair.

The End

Regret at parting.
The coming of morning.
The drumming of the rain.
How cold the house becomes.
How cold the day.
Seeping wishes wished and dead.
If only one lover regrets the parting,
can this aubade still be an aubade?

Disenchantment

Balled breaths of cottenwood whiffle about
my head, against the high, sun-fluttered leaves

and leaves low and dark, touched by seeping night.
Now, the wind is less than stir, it's a pass,

a slow-eyed aim, the wake of a planet
sick of its circles and keeping a vow

to leave that grave-dug rut; a criminal
comet vowing to flee, not left nor right;

straining straight for something green and living
and safe.

Happy Hiding

A bird trembles in the middle of Beech
Street. Did she read the sign and dream of trees:
Peach, apple, pear? She found just a yellow
Stripe striping the blacktop hot in the sun,
Sparkling in deep night with the lights of cars.
But the bird – a barn-orphaned swallow – flicks
Her head in the middle of Beech Street
And trees – peach, apple, pear – bubble up
With shade. And a happy hiding in leaves.

In a Forty-Ninth Street Coffee Shop

The city saves a sooty dusk
for this middle of its noise.
In the glooming of the buildings
through the gritty windows
her paper waitress-hat loses its light.
The woman's eyes take
something burned
from the air, dust the edges,
and arouse hope
in the man who drinks
the coffee she brings.
She's meant, he thought,
for other places,
other people,
higher graces.
But what *she* wants
he never learns.
He never asks
for what she yearns.
He only drinks
the coffee she brings;
and steps out
into the bus-ugly dark
leaving on the table
a quarter and a dime.

Razing the Dead

The building climbed a hundred years
ago and housed a century of families.

But, now echoes and dust
settle on the rotted wood.

The bricks crumble; windows long
broken from pitched rocks

and picking tramps. The building looks
like a holey used-up ticket

the conductor has punched
for one last ride on the train.

Subway

The Lexington Avenue Local bumps
south; standers sway over sitters and not
one looks at another one, yet each sees.
In a corner sits Austin, beneath the red
panic cord waving in the waving car.
His eyes flicker behind thick glasses.
At each stop, he tips into not hearing.
His head is bald (with hair like lines we make
coaxing a pen to write). The sitters
and the standers step in and step out,
and the red knob of the panic brake bobs
at the end of its rope. Austin squints, showing
yellowed dentures. He can't snatch the name
of the station out of the clack and roar
in the electric cave. It's fifty-ninth street he wants.
The train stops there, opens its rusty doors
to the odors of grease and gross. Austin
breaths through his mouth and aims his squint out
the window. *Watch the closing doors...* cuts through
the understreet all, just as he spots
the tiled "Fifty-Nine." "My stop!" Austin spits,
"My stop!" The standers and sitters pack tight.
But from somewhere within them an arm clamps
the edge of the slicing door and holds it
firm and open. Austin forces his frown
between those who won't look and steps on
the grit platform. He pats the hand before

it releases the door. He wheezes a smile,
"Thank you, brother." The door closes, the train
lurches, ignoring on. And through a sooty
scratched window no one sees Austin wave.

Roles

On the train I am a poet
breaking lines along the line.
In the city I am a walker
and a talker and a drudge,
stepping on the shadows
of the buildings on the street.

Mind Reading

What does the snow know?
Does it swirl and dart smart?
Will it choose to cover or hover
       To seek the coldest bed?

Can it make the wind rescind
What its first thought sought
In the crystal-washed tumbling and fumbling
       That grayed the sky with dread?

Quite Close

Horizon stars and fireflies
Never stray far from earth.
The moon-blued night of darkened arms
Bears silver light in birth
Above the hill-bound trees.

To float and flit and dot the dark
With bubbles that won't burst.
In keeping close, the stars and flies
Are practiced and well-versed
And feel quite close to me.

Holy Summer

The tree gives limb and leaf
To the thrush, to the squirrel
And shade to me.
Shade, stories in the wind,
And etchings against the sky.
I give ear to the thrush,
Smile to the squirrel
And worship –
beneath its branches –
To the tree.

Nor Myth

Finch sighs at all the fenders and rusted
cans from forty years ago on the banks

of Killbuck Creek. Posts pull pointless barbed-wire
down to the weeds. How is it he *sees* two

young souls sitting on a grassed hill over
Annville looking down on the road along

Killbuck Creek? The soul of the girl is May,
her ghost smiles in his thoughts. Finch is the soul

of the boy. There is no wind, no cooling
above May's father's farm. On that soft hill

they sit higher than the silo. Like stalled
birds, a swallow, a wren. They're quiet, caught

young and holding hands. The thrumming of cars
and dump-trucks below dies as it tries to rise

to them on the hill. And May's eyes ripple
as she speaks of her father's cows milked down

and sold from a hundred to a few to none.
And how now her father lives his gray days

simply oiling things. Her mother prefers
sleep to church. Why, wonders Finch, are there no

myths to call upon to rescue hilltop
hope when such shadows seep into his thinking?

Why is there no crown, no chorus, no jeweled sword,
no swooning? There is only a village

six miles downroad – sotted and needing paint.
Finch climbed the hill where he sits with May, climbed

out of the village, out of the fumes to sit
with May high over Killbuck Creek. He stopped

asking how the season could leave, how May
could flee and how he could slip away.
From the hill. From Annville. From May. And now
only wisps without myth are left to sit

holding hands on a hill over Annville
young, caught in thought from forty years ago.

Second Cutting

Straw-hatted hayers are mowing the hay today.
Sun bakes it all stick-brittle brown
and it settles with the settling wind.
Autumn's on prowl through a ring of beeches
lighting the blighted field; the air cools blue
and empty. The hayers hoard the yellow
and green in the grey mow. Does a woodchuck,
I am wond'ring, or a mussed-up boy peek
between the splintered slats and grieve unseen
by the hayers? Does a sunburned seer
know the day for clover-play is near done,
cut, crushed and giving up its ghostly smell
to a spider spinning her web in their work?

Resignation

We can aspire to a thing higher
than dreams of them beside us.
And the sheer height and heat
Will lift us up to giddiness.
But a cooling, calming catch
will set us down again
down to where we know despair...
We're aged, lined, sorrowed, drifted,
too weak to rise again.

Savannah

In a bookstore a powdered woman drawled
directions through three blocks to the Crystal

Beer Parlour. The sky in front of me was blue
with cigar smoke clouds all a-grumble

and plotting rain. Spanish moss trembled 'neath
the trees, which did weave with the leaves and lay

across an election sign for candidate
Billy Hair. I came upon the tavern

as the storm came upon the town. The tin
ceilings were high and dark as the outside

sky. Slow pull-chain fans breathed a lazy breeze
on the wooden booths. Outside, day gusted

and rain rapped on the window. Lightning burned
the air to an ozone smell. Inside, in the dark

and fanning air, I smelled the smell of beer
thrilling at the grand storm and loving it.

Obituary

This scarlet-painted wooden store rises
At the edge of the road. I cross a strip
of lawn and climb the steps into sweet smells:
Cinnamon and syrup, jars with candy
Sticks, gold leaf boxes of milk chocolates,
Brown bread seeded and dewing its plastic
Wrappers, jars of chutney and relish with
Hand-printed labels. I squeeze past an old
Woman who turns at my *Excuse me.* She
Wears a gray dress (even its flowers) and
Squints up at me. I browse past her and head
Out of the odors and up a worn step
To the next room where mason jars and steel
Dippers glint with the sunshine shafting through
The window and with the flourescent blue
Glow above. Here cookie cutters, tea pots,
And plates with green scenes beckon from Japan.
The next room, the next step up shows this store
Is surely not small. I find socks, fuzzy
Brown gloves, and mufflers muffling the talk.
The squinting old woman, with her white hair
Straight over her ears, scuffs my way, turning
And nudging between mothers and children
And men in red flannel shirts by tables
Of back-scratchers, walls of neckties, boxes
Of flat, black wallets. She presses her hand
As she shuffles closer, on magnetic
Money clips, cat calendars, leg-warmers,

And shirts with scenes of golden retrievers
With or without ducks in their mouths. I slip
Into the little book room farther back,
Another step up and off to the left.
I tilt my head and search along the shelves:
Ah, Books about snowflakes, Calvin Coolidge,
And moths. My way to the next aisle is blocked
By the old woman, now scratching a rash
On her arm and still wrinkling cloudy eyes
Through bifocles.

Is your name Leonard? she dabs at her chin
With a hanky.

No. I look away and wonder how could Anyone
fill a whole book with Calvin Coolidge.

You look like a fella I knew, name of
Leonard.

Well, I'm not.

You sure look like him.

Where's he live?

He don't. He died back in the seventies.
Over in Ludlow.

The old woman spits Leonard's death notice,
Sniffs and huffs out of the book room. Her black
Shoes are heavy-heeled. I watch her scrape on
Her way and I forget about Calvin
Coolidge. I'm thinking of Leonard and how
Much I look like a dead man.

Rain and a Bank

How did these rocks
Come to this place –
Blasted, sliced, cut, chipped,
Hauled, mortared, pushed, wedged?
In a straight dropping rain
The bank's granite blocks soak
at the bottom to a darker stone-grey.
On the windows the rain
Moves like seance beads
Lighted by flourescents
Over the counters.
The bankers and banking
Jiggle through the curtain.
Inside light glows from blue
Rectangles flat against the ceiling;
Stronger than the day
Soaking at the bottom
To a dark stone-grey.

Quarrel

Under sunshine (and clouds
like a dinosaur spine)
two crows squabble
in the shuddering
August maples.
The breeze
flutters in mischief.
I am puzzled by the dispute,
not knowing the crows.
But it's brief
and done
and morning is handed back
to grasshoppers,
to leaves,
and to me.

Shush the Shoes

Creak of leather,
Slap of sandal
Sneaker squeak
Good, hard clack of cordovan heel.

Scuffing, trudging
Walkers announce their approach:
A leather creak,
A sneaker squeak
The good, hard clack of a cordovan heel.

Book Care

I saunter through the bookstore door
to visit my book on the bookstore shelf.
There it sits: small and green
There it sits: right in between
Eliot and Robert Frost.

I go for a visit, quite often, I do.
To stand that little book straight
Between Rob and Thomas
To heighten any promise
My sweet book might have.

I'll not let the little volume lean
Or grow dusty and musty or droop.
But, I have a bit of concern
About its home for which I yearn
And dream and sigh and pray.

My book's been there long enough
To know Eliot and Frost by first name.
I trust it shows great courtesy
So if in my visit I were to see
My book chatting with Tom and Rob.

It looks, I fear, a little thin
And its cover's beginning to curl.
Can't they hold the humid air
Between a sweat and a Frigidaire?

To keep the poems comfy?

I am impressed and proud of the company:
Tom and Rob are solid and thick
Hardback, hard-nosed, hard-sold
Well-told, so bold, pure gold.
They don't sport a single curl.

My small book is young and frail
Growing in the womb of my mind
It doesn't know how to be
Out in the world, now that it's free
And on its rhyming, climbing own.

I wish my tome would find a nice home
And leave the bookstore shelf.
Oh, perhaps, the cottage of a pretty wife
Enchanted by literary life
Sipping tea in the prosodic eve.

Her hubby would smile through pipe smoke
At the sight of her reading my words.
She'd sigh and raise her gaze
To the ceiling through the haze
Or out their lilaced window.

They'd have a pup, brown and snoring
And lying at her feet. A pup whose sleep
Would cease when the wife responds
To the trees and meadows and ponds
Sitting, waiting in my leafy pages.

I turn from these ministrations
To the clerk who pipes, "May I help you?"
And drop my eyes to the table displaying
Children's books and games for playing
And pictures and puzzles, all selling well.

"Just looking," I lie, 'fore adding a "Thanks."
But I want to say, to wring my hands
And plead, "Please, please, please
For the love of Cummings, seize
My book and whisk it up front!

"To stand displayed and inviting.
Beside the CD chanting enchantment
Out of your bookstore amplifier
To inspire someone to be the buyer
Of my humble, little book.

Take the delicate thing. Hold it up,
Let the light play on its deep green front
And show how it sits with grace
In the hand, in the eye and heart place
Where lyrics lift and roll and sing."

But, my time with my book
On the bookstore shelf comes to a book end
And out I go from the telling, retailing store
Leaving behind all the stories and lore…
And I think I hear my little book cry.

What I Know

This is what I know of heaven:
It is a tree. It is trees upon hills.
Trees upon hills that claw the clouds
To shreds of fog to jewel the needles and leaves.
It is a bird. It is birds.
Robins. Warblers. Swallows. Wrens.
Red-winged blackbirds to glisten and flit.
Heaven is a hayfield. It is hayfields rising to the hill.
Hayfields greening with the hill trees.
Greening. Then, golding. Waving in the wind.
Heaven is wind. It is winds. Speaking secrets.
Speaking secrets from lifting shadows
And looking underneath for ghosts.
Ghosts for stories. Ghosts for teaching
Of what will be.

What I Saw This Morning

An angel bounced to icy earth
and feather-tossed the snow
up, up in the knoll-top trees.
An old angel whose tired
wing-muscle tone sighed,
trembled, froze, and failed.
From what? From the weight
of keeping young?
Of keeping the young served,
happy, entertained by worship?
Did this angel drop and lose altitude
from his eye-hoping attitude
that the young will come
into a sagging sanctuary,
out of cold and snow and wind?
the angel fell to icy earth
as hope for the young fell...
that they would come
and keep the faith.

Aunt Tillie's Garden

From the pipe in the stone fount water gasps
Into wind, stringing its dotty vapor
To the peony trellis while lilacs
And moss beard the walls of the old clapboard
Cottage. On a pole, a birdhouse teeters
Empty as the amber beer bottles flicked
By the gravel road in the bent, brown grass.
Scarred and gray and splintered croquet balls rot
Beside a willow stump. And from the house,
With paint split and curling, a radio
Keens for a girl who wrote a note to say
She's leaving home. The song threads the screen door,
through the cotton wad on guard against flies.

Barred

Eagle street started narrow 'neath maples
and elms back in those sad, grayed days of war

between the states. It stayed narrow well on
into the honking nights of black autos

and jazz, when neon first lighted Annville
and street lamps floated high up in the trees,

haloing the leaves with a small heaven,
never settled to the ground, to the town,

to air smelling of cigarettes and sweat.
Standing on the asphalt, his hand glass-cold

and his head spinning in uncaught thought,
a man, any man – chaf-dusted farmer;

ex-soldier bent and grayed with wounded-weight;
a mechanic with an unwanted child –

any fellow can still see Eagle street
narrows up ahead, narrows and closes.

Would the eye lie? Even an eye scratched
with blood? No. Eagle street ends up ahead.

No way out there. So, a fellow always
turns away, turns away and follows the fumes

to the amber crazed bottom of a clear-
glass mug. Eagle Street ends with no way out.

Sanctuary

Through the stained glass window you see little
puffs of dirt on the sign pointing to Steamburg,
crossed with one showing the way to Randolph.
In this Methodist church, in the middle
of a hamlet in farmed and faraway
western New York I sit waiting to worship.
The corner of the purple hymnal
in the rack on the back of the pew
in front of me is split and shows its cardboard
core. I try to meditate, to contemplate,
before they pass the plate and ask for noisy
coins. Sounds ride in the peeling sanctuary:
the crack of the winter-weary wood; sniffs
and blows of old people noses under
eyes clouded against some sun-colored
heaven riding a line from the windows
to the floor. The sniffers breathe work-weary
breaths. They step up the steps a step at a time,
leaning on their canes and cares, coming
to this clapboard church that tries to stay painted
and fails. As I sit waiting to worship
I hear tardy cars rattle the gravel
out in the lot. Do they think, I wonder,
in the brief struggle it is to get out
of their cars, about raising money
for asphalt? Do they think, I wonder,
in the brief struggle it is to climb the steps,
about raising money for concrete?

Is the thought of patching this crumbling church
left in the vestibule with those thoughts
of somebody else's wife? Or how much
beer *was* it last night? I sit waiting
to worship and try to picture the pastor
off in a back room putting on his faith.
He'll enter to sing and preach and pray
rounded down in his heavy, ironed robe.
From the sniffs and stirring I look out
through the yellow glass dedicated
to remembering a forgot farmer,
I look out at maples and an arthritic
orchard on a rock-pocked knoll. I look out
at a field where snow has bent and broken
the hay. Nothing now pushes up through
the dirt and the earth in this field by the church;
no cutting to go into the leaning
grey barn, where the last cow was sold blurred years
ago. Beside the church, beside the road, a sign
points to Steamburg and crosses with another
pointing to Randolph. And I sit. I sit.
I sit. Waiting in silence to worship.

One Valley Visit

Night and a soft breeze.
Two shadows rise in the moon
And a street lamp glows
Upon the windows and leaves.
We circle the rusty structure
And sit in the playground swing.
All around are the wooded hills
That make a little valley.
A school at night is good to visit.
A maple tree stands in front
While ivy grips the bricks.
The maple stands free.
Both school and tree loom proud;
Wisdom is where it will be witnessed.
No thing should inanimate be assessed.

Quite Close

Horizon stars and fireflies
Never stray far from earth.
The moon-blued night of darkened arms
Bears silver light in birth
Above the hill-bound trees.

To float and flit and dot the dark
With bubbles that won't burst.
In keeping close, the stars and flies
Are practiced and well-versed
And feel quite close to me.

Lost

That moon *you* see,
I see, too.
Through your branches,
Through mine.
That moon, that one moon
Glowing over
Different lawns and porches
Was the moon
Under which we kissed
Under which a moment
Lifted ...velvet
...gone.

Parting

Let it hurt,
hit your heart,
a pierce, a ping.
Let it sing
and whisper leaves
on summer eaves
that speak of rain
and the insane
sorrow of parting.
Tomorrow starting
for miles and years
for sighs and fears
for hope failing,
trailing, wailing
in your hurt heart.

Inlander at the Atlantic

The ocean gasps
on the rocks
outside my window.

Pleading voices;
dying voices;
voices spirited away,

raggéd and spent
from a far place.
The broken distance,

the strangled wave,
a frothing failing,
fades their words;

pushes them down;
and caps their loss
with foam.

Nothing New

The poet leaves a poem.
The soldier leaves a corpse.

Nineteen Sixty-Nine

Ha! Court blares on the White House lawn
...like the mud dent of a dying alligator.

Who's To Say

Why, you could climb the wrinkles
on his face and reach,
with your eyes,
The black campaign cap
and *V.F.W.* in yellow letters.

Old Man Grantley is long back
from something.
Something killing.

Too damn many beers
have blasted his capillaries
and bulged his belly.
Cigarettes have lowered
the give of his lungs.

He always claims he was lucky
when he jaws about the war.
But who's to say
he ever came back?
Ever came back
from battle.

Fin de Siecle

A late century
snow-
fall.
Old win-
ter waxy
flakes in
the orange
light
of night
glowing
quaint
and leaving.

Frosted Thread

We see the night,
the window mirrored,
sucking up our talking.

It cools, it falls,
it carries down the sound
of all our walking.

Oh, night may come
and air may freeze
and winter fill the moment

with something begging
to be seen and felt and killing.
There is no warming boat,

no heating up or leaving
this pulling down,
this shivered frown,
this frosted thread,
this weaving.

I Wish I Knew Your Name

With your wild, beckoning hair
you look like an old movie lover.
Black and white and hazed
in the soft, silent
uncrossed distance of years.
And the empty room between us.
I cannot step back to then
Just as I cannot mount
A ragged line of lightning
and run from here to heaven;
nor can we powder in the thunder
to be pure, loud sound.
To reach you in your there
I cannot rein in the warm rain
to fall upon this churched earth
that is holy with hope and seed
and root and risings and lives.

In Omne Tempus

Through the pub window
thrums a summer rain
plunking the car roof
exploding, tumbling
down in a hundred
pummeling storms that
weave a dark sparking
grayness into June's
sweet green. So I find
the hundred little
storms through the pub glass.
I'm thrilled and I pray
the rain will fall forever.

What Do You Make of the Bard?

You'll find you'll *shake*
As you train your *ear*
On words you take
From the name *Shakespeare*.

It's fleshed with fruit:
Did Lear taste a *pear*?
In this pursuit
At the end all *are*.

On the Thames dock
Did Will fish for *hakes*?
Did bright Shylock
Know *pe* for land's sakes?

Perhaps some mean
You're seeming to see?
Like sick ol' Greene,
Color of a *pea*.

What more to make
Of the name *Shakespeare*?
Your heart might *ake*
From loss of your dear.

Jul'et hushed Romeo
With "*sh*" 'neath the night,

So would Will know
A*ha*! At word just right.

And in the middle
Is how Will could see
Through a riddling riddle:
Blessed, you see, with *e.s.p.*

Photograph

I saw an old poet
wading in the
hay and English daisies
of a Dymock field.
He had hiked there
when he was young
and wording poems;
when his love and
children were alive.
Clouds drag the hills
with rolling shadows,
from hedge-row
to the valley grass,
tumbling to rest
beneath the trees.
The poet thinks
of his wife,
of his children,
and of a Welsh poet
killed in war.
Does he see them all
in the broken shade
beneath the trees?
Is coming here
in so large a stride of time
a stick
that stirs the grief
time had banked.

He puts a hand over his eyes
and cries.
I saw it
in a photograph.

Exorcising Sorrow and Attending to Grief

Give away that chalice a holy man
gave you.
Smell the fur of a dog.
Or a rabbit.
Listen to the wind through the bare winter maple.
Listen to the wind in a spring pine.
Listen to the wind shushing the summer willow.
Take autumn off and just look.
Hear the creak of winter in the wood of your house.
Hear the creak of winter under the ice
In its muffled capillary pulse.
Walk up and down a dirt road.
Pray to blue shadows in the snow.
Think about ducks.
Think about one duck.
Stare into the eyes of a dog.
Or a rabbit.
Be happy for squirrels.
Be happy for one squirrel.
Cry.
Listen to leaves crackling underfoot.
Speak of fish
And wear a green scarf.
Put your hand on a warm shoulder.
Act calm.
Advise calm.
Counsel calm.

Be calm.
Make a sound with your mouth.
Feel with your hand
the fabric of the chair where you sit.
Reach down from that chair
in hope
you'll find
the fur of a dog.

Goodbye, Annville

Goodbye, Lutie, Mr. Felton, Buffie Burnmark and Uncle Clyde.
Goodbye, Margie's Diner —vanilla cokes and fish fries.
Goodbye, maple trees with leaves like frozen, green smoke.
Goodbye, "Monday, Monday."
> *I stop somewhere new and still wait for you.*

Goodbye, clumpy clouded, rumbling thunderstorms.
Goodbye, triangle park across Fair Oak Street and the Rock
    City Hotel.
Goodbye, foggy, feathered air on Cattaraugus creek.
> *Houses and rooms are full of perfumes.*

Goodbye, Schwinn bike and mothered-bad-haircuts.
Goodbye, elderly twins, Hammer and Handle.
Goodbye to that "...god-damned Rockefeller!"
> *I cannot be shaken but I can be taken.*

Goodbye, red-winged blackbird.
Goodbye, Peachie the barber and Huckleberry Finn.
Goodbye and thanks for oily butter and photos from the Civil War.
> *My left hand's placed around your waist.*

Let me lie down between that old canvas pup tent
And the fairgrounds grandstand.
From this moment forward the ban on baseball after dark …
    is lifted.

Ira Joe Fisher

Ira Joe Fisher was raised in the charming western New York village of Little Valley. His poetry has appeared in *Poetry New York*, *The Alembic*, *The New York Quarterly*, *Entelechy International*, *Diner*, *Ridgefield Magazine*, *The New Hampshire Review* and the anthology *Confrontation*. He is the author of several verse collections and a book of essays. Ira presents readings and conducts poetry workshops in New York and throughout New England. He has a Master of Fine Arts degree in poetry from New England College and has taught poetry, communications and broadcast history there. He has taught poetry and creative writing at the University of Connecticut, Stamford, and Mercy University in Dobbs Ferry, New York, and Founders Hall in Ridgefield. Ira has lectured at Manhattanville College and Keene State College in New Hampshire.

In June of 2023, Fisher was named Poet Laureate of Ridgefield, Connecticut.

Ira is a member of SAG/AFTRA and Actors' Equity. He regularly performed in the long-running musical *The Fantasticks* for five years. He appeared in the musical *The Prince and the Pauper* at New York City's Lambs Theatre. And as "Monsignor Buckley" in the reader's theatre drama *The Garden of Dromore* at the New York University Hot Ink Festival. Ira also acted in the film "California Girls" and in the ABC daytime drama "Loving." He was a regular on the CBS *Early Show*.

Ira and his wife, Shelly, live in Ridgefield.